By Art Boericke and Barry Shapiro

Handmade Houses
A Guide to the Woodbutcher's Art
The Craftsman Builder

The CRAFTSMAN BUILDER

ART BOERICKE & BARRY SHAPIRO

A FIRESIDE BOOK
PUBLISHED BY SIMON AND SCHUSTER

First Fireside Edition, 1979
Published by Simon and Schuster A Division of Gulf & Western Corporation Simon & Schuster Building Rockefeller Center
1230 Avenue of the Americas New York, New York 10020

Designed by Susan Sherry Shapiro
Manufactured in the United States of America
1 2 3 4 5 6 7 8 9 10
1 2 3 4 5 6 7 8 9 10 Pbk.

Library of Congress Cataloging in Publication Data

Boericke, Art.
The craftsman builder.

(A Fireside book)
1. House construction—Pictorial works. I. Shapiro, Barry,
joint author. II. Title.
TH4812.B63 1977b 690'.8 79-13829

ISBN 0-671-22818-8
ISBN 0-671-25192-9 Pbk.

*Without the financial support of Family and Friends; and
the technical assistance of Mr. Mike Phillips & Mr. Joel Hukins
of Nikon Inc., this volume would not have been possible in its present form.
We would also like to thank Alan Kahn.*

Preface

I SUPPOSE THAT the job itself is a better teacher than we generally admit, for a lot of people who have migrated to sparsely settled parts of the western states have suddenly become mighty fine craftsmen. Just take a single look at these homes, these barns, these greenhouses. They're serviceable, they're solid, and they've got style!

Yet the carpenters who built them are so randomly scattered and so different from one another in so many respects (young and not so young, naive and sophisticated, middle and working class, women and men, gay and straight, white and black, radical and conservative, churchgoing and totally unaffiliated) that they seem to have only one thing in common: a single-mindedness that will see them through all kinds of rugged rural employment—and also through some pretty tough winters. For you can't build anything at all if you can't make it through a Cascade, a Big Horn, or a New Mexican winter.

But if this dogged rural endurance isn't purely an out-West phenomenon, this kind of quality construction is. And it's happening in an area twice that of Texas, and ten times as varied as the whole Eastern Seaboard. For out here you may have to settle on parched desert soils, or in dank, mossy forests; and you may have to take root where the summers are 120 degrees in the shade or the winters 40 below year after year!

However that may be—regardless of the site and its difficulties, and despite the fact that even top-notch owner-built homes have had very little money behind them—a good many of them have taken on a well-tended almost affluent look. But fat-bellied or lean, I'd say that the real changes in craftsmanship are the result of a curious, unique sort of merging—a newfangled do-si-do, a funky sashaying of all sorts of building and craft intuitions midst hundreds of high-stepping, wide-awake settlers.

Now if you think that these notions about "craft intuitions" are a little farfetched, consider that only a few years ago migrant Indians, trappers, and miners slogged down these valleys, skirted these jagged, cold mountains, crossed these same giant swift-flowing rivers. And right behind them the first settlers followed, came and built barns and fences and houses. But when they'd finished their labors, not one of this pioneer lot had achieved much in the way of a well-thought-out, well-crafted homestead—only an occasional barn or a fence that you could point to with pride.

Today those who are just newly arrived and, increasingly, their native-born neighbors *are* creating a style. For they are bringing a snap and a zing to their work as they adapt *everything*, every last bit of their construction—terraces, fences, outhouses, pergolas—to the climate, the slope, the feel of the land. Just look right here at the way they use wood, and the way they use stone. At the way they use concrete, glass, adobe, and tile. Yes, they have intuitive flashes all right, but it's mainly hard work—a lot of experimenting and a lot of adjusting to get things to look right, to get things to fit.

Yet whether it takes two, three or seventeen years, they are doing the job as it has to be done. They are doing what's called for. And they are trusting each other to develop the skills that build into structures an appropriate spirit or style. They are trusting each other in much the same way that I trusted my students to build a good sturdy place in wet, windswept marshlands.

Assembled here are the first chapters of this new western saga. A photo-journal of the strong, cheap, joyous, neighborly dwellings that dot our dry chaparral, our dark, tangled woodlands and long, verdant valleys. Buildings that speak softly of the days and hours, the sweat and tears that make them an imaginative and beautiful part of this landscape.

And dwellings that house bright-eyed, exuberant builders as well—house their belongings, their tables and chairs, their tools and kitchenware, their beds, guns, and guitars. And their growing, everyday, rural American pride, a pride in things made with their hands.

Art Boericke

THIS COZY, comfortable country home, built from wine tanks, took three craftsmen builders eighteen months to complete, whereas suburban tract homes take six weeks at the most. You get what you pay for—in time, as well as money.

THIS COUPLE'S budget didn't allow them to use more than a single layer of ferro-cement—hence a sheet-metal stove where the small fireplace would usually do. And though it might appear so, the thin skin is hardly fireproof.

THE CO-AUTHOR of *Mud, Space, and Spirit* makes fireplace building as much a sculptor's art as a builder's craft; and her new addition is a lot more interesting and snug than many an older adobe—though they were generally a high point in early Southwest building.

IN THE NORTHWEST, where the skies are frequently dark or gray for weeks on end, rough white plaster makes a very serviceable and reflective interior surface—while keeping out the damp.

YES, just one post is holding up that ridge piece. That's the basic structure. All of it!

GREAT WORK begins with an intuitive idea perhaps, but each
and every detail must be crafted to enhance it. Indeed, "quality" is not
something divisible or added on, as one of Canada's finest builders
amply demonstrates in his woodland cabin.

A VERY SOPHISTICATED use of mud and bricks, and one where the traditional vigas and latias are even more strongly emphasized than in the older New Mexican homes.

THIS HANDSOME STRUCTURE will be partially heated by a pretty bathroom tub which is designed to store hot water from an adjacent building's solar panels. This innovation not only adds a new function to the bathroom's mundane chores; it also makes its sporadic use for fun and bathing more economic too.

A SERIES of doors and shuttered windows opening out to an endless view and river-fed breezes may give the exterior of this Colorado hexagon a somewhat calculated look; but craftsmanship and a lot of imagination sure keep things whirling once you're inside.

PAUL AND GINNY SOLDNER: Three buildings and twenty years of experimenting have got things exactly right here.

PART OF IT IS finding the proper feeling for a beam's placement, its proportion, or its height or girth. Another part is using materials that improve with age instead of those that deteriorate or fall apart. And possibly it helps to be an artist too.

LIKE THE SCRAP METAL transformed by this famous artist-craftsman into tools and sculpture—certain types of salvaged or unmilled wood are usually free; but first you have to find them, and then learn how to use them.

THERE IS, by the way, a small open conduit up there on the kitchen ceiling which pulls warm air into the bedroom by means of a discarded vacuum cleaner fan. A B.T.U. saved is a B.T.U. earned!

ONE OF THE high-water marks in twentieth-century craftsmanship is this group of buildings—the workshops, studio, and living quarters for an artist and his family. Everything has been done by the artist himself or by an occasional part-time apprentice.

DESPITE EACH BUILDING being built with varying materials and varying types of intensity and rhythm, an extraordinary unity has been achieved, particularly with the stark, gently rolling hills and the wind-carved trees.

VOLUME THREE will include the sixth and most complex building in this undertaking—looming up now, partially complete, on the far side of the pool.

THIS BUILDER learned his stone-laying from a Spanish-speaking mason, and his economic use of space from several years spent with Navajo Indians. Thus he has made a handsome, durable double-walled home that is small and tight enough to withstand the desert's bright, cold autumn days, winter blizzards, and savage April winds.

BELIEVE IT OR NOT: a two-hundred-dollar sturdy, tight, well-lit log home!

A PAINTER'S STUDIO where an absolutely focused and unwavering concentration has brought to its floors and walls the same qualities of attentive craftsmanship that mark the giant mandala opposite his bed.

COMING UP in the next volume—its giant shakes and bent poles towering more than twenty feet above the children's heads—is the greatest wood-frame building in the U.S.A. I'm sure the kids think so, and so do I.

Credits,
Acknowledgments,
& Afterthoughts

A FEW OF US continue to build with whatever we can scrounge or come by in any manner—preferring the worn, antique look provided by reuse and ingenuity. But this somewhat time-consuming, extravagant technique has steadily declined, partly because of the lack of suitable materials (compare, for example, my own home, pages 8–11 of *Handmade Houses*, which uses top-grade maple flooring on a kitchen wall, with Alexander Weygers' more economical use of unmilled but tightly fitted vertical slabs for exterior siding, this volume, page 53).

Indeed, in almost every case now, earlier building methods have been followed or paralleled by ones that display both greater craftsmanship and greater originality. This is true both in the handling of newer materials such as concrete and ferro-cement, and in the handling of older, more traditional materials such as adobe, stained glass, stucco, and plaster.

Yet while Barry and I certainly tried—it took us six months and 15,000 miles to put together this book—we could not come up with the best or the most definitive examples of every system of building; that goes without saying. I hope, therefore, that readers will feel free to send us photos of the homes of their friends and, for that matter, will feel free to suggest ways to make our almanacs more complete or comprehensive—but kindly note that a self-addressed envelope will help things along, as I haven't anyone to help with the mail.

Admittedly, some excellent places that we've heard of or seen remain unphotographed. In the first place, an unseasonable August was against us in the Pacific Northwest and in Canada. In the second place, to be selected at all, a home had to be viewable from a number of angles—both inside and out—for our primary concern is that each place be able to tell its own story with little or no editorial comment.

Virginia Gray was a great, a very great help, both as a guide to New Mexico and as a judge of places outside her home state. If enough public interest is shown in this series, then both the work load and the burden of appraising new places can be more equally shared. If your home is in this new volume you ought to help select the homes for future volumes—that is, if you feel inclined to do so, and I hope that many of you will.

It has been a real pleasure not only to meet so many outstanding builder-craftsmen, but also to be so courteously received by so many persons who were, naturally, hard pressed for time, country life being what it is. Unfortunately, a list of our many, many guides, hosts, informants, and diverse entertainers will have to wait for the next book and more space.

Nonetheless we wish to thank you personally, one and all, and to comment in closing that on no occasion did anyone whose home appears herein propose their own place to us—quite the contrary. Time and time again, instead of their own homes, builders and architects proposed those of friends or passing acquaintances—an indication, I think, of the generous spirit that is an essential part of those who have achieved some real fundamental success in their own building programs.

Owners & Craftsmen